The Glow Up Recovery Plan

Dedication

I dedicate this book to my one and only **Madison Rose**. You are so patient, kind, loving, and artistic. Every day you are my voice of reason and the only reason I never give up. I could not imagine my life without you, because I have you I have something to live for and look forward to waking up every morning to put a smile on your face. As you grow older I want you to never forget that mommy loves you best.

To my mother **Amy Dean**, I love you until infinity. You are always my voice of reason. It does not matter if I'm right or wrong, I know one thing for certain and two things for sure my mommy will ride for me. Thank you for always pushing me to be great and believing in me when at times I do not believe in myself.

To my dearest friend **Woukly**, I love you girl you are always there for me in more ways than one. Every time I come to you with an idea or something I want to do, I know if you can help you are right there ready to do whatever. You are so business savvy and if I do not have it, you always say don't worry I'll invest. If plan A don't work out, I know you always have my back ready to come through as my plan B. This is a forever thing no miles can come between us.

To my sister friend **Ashley Bell;** thank you for listening to me rant and rave every morning. I think for the past five years, you're one of the few people I talk to everyday and about everything. I truly believe that God brought our parents together, so he can bring us together. I don't care where in the world you go, you will FOREVER be my sister.

To my big brothers **Samir, Eric, Wes, Bub, Telly and Michael;** thank you for always being there for me when I call. If I do not know anything, I know my brothers are one call away no matter the cost, miles, or time. You all are there for me in your own ways.

I want to thank my dad, **Floyd Anderson**; he put his life on hold for me for approximately two years just to come stay with me and help me out with my daughter when I needed it the most. My dad is the strongest man I know. He's a three-time cancer survivor and through each surgery, I was by his side except for the last. When I called him to let him know that I was not going to be able to be present for this last surgery, he did not hit me with a guilt trip he simply said, "I understand baby girl." He goes above and beyond doing the smallest things so that I will not be stressed out and for that your baby girl will forever ride with you.

Finally, I want to thank my **Aunt Tots** and all five of my sister cousins; **Nakia, Leslie, Wendy, Tia,** and **Tunisia.** Because of you guys I'm a better woman I learned different things about owning and being me from each of you over the years and I just want to say thank you for dropping jewels and giving me tough love even when I do not understand it at times.

Growth is painful Change is painful, but nothing is as painful as staying stuck somewhere you don't belong.
-Narayana Murthy

Personal Information

This Glow Up Recovery Plan Belongs to:

Name: _____

Address: _____

City: _____ State: _____ Zip:_____

Telephone: _____

Email: _____

Special Instructions: _____

_____

_____

_____

_____

What Is a Glow Up Recovery Plan?

This is a self-management and recovery book to provide you with positive ways to cope with the curve balls of life. This book is designed to help you when you are struggling with difficult situations in life. It will assist you in:

- Decreasing stress
- Increasing self-awareness and self-Empowerment
- Improve the quality of life

This book is to help you monitor uncomfortable situations and emotions to assist in reducing stress and emotions that arise from different life events. You can use the tools in this book as often as you'd like and whenever you feel the need. You do not have to use every tool but utilize the tools that apply to the situation at hand. As you flip through the pages and complete the different exercises pay attention to the exercises that resonate with things that occurred in the past and would have been helpful at that time. Utilize the exercise in the book to help prepare yourself for stressful situations that may or may not occur in your life. I ask that you highlight those pages, mark the page, put an asterisk on that page, or do whatever that will help you remember to go back to that particular page when life hands you lemons and you have to make lemonade.

How to Use The Glow Up Recovery Plan?

You will use this book to help you make lemonade out of the lemons that life will bring. In order for this book to be effective, you will have to take about ten to fifteen minutes out of your day to review and be willing to take action when needed. This is just a suggestion. You are more than welcome to go at your own pace. You may find that you don't need every exercise, or every chapter may not apply to your life at this very moment. My suggestion is at some point you complete the exercise anyway so when or if the situation occurs, you are prepared.

When you become comfortable with your Glow Up Recovery Plan, you will find that you will not have to review the book as often. Please start at the beginning of this book to get the full effect but feel free to skip through pages and start where you feel the need.

And please remember this book is not to replace therapy. If you feel that you honestly need a therapist or need to talk to someone regarding your feelings and emotions, please contact a therapist. You can use this book in conjunction with your therapy sessions.

Note: *Throughout this book I will include some self-disclosure. Self-disclosure is a therapeutic technique used in therapy where the therapist will disclose something about themselves or their personal life to a client to show support, build rapport, or normalize a situation. I'm disclosing to show you that I have went through hard times too; I have dealt with an array of emotions and life situations. And at times I felt stuck but using these exercise/tools have helped me glow through everything I go through.*

When we are no longer able to change a situation, we are challenged to change ourselves.
-Viktor E. Frankl

It's Some Changes I've Been Going Through

The above quote helps you understand a little about life. Well when I read it, that is what I took from it. When I first read the quote, I was going through a really tough time. I always dealt with change, especially drastic change in a hard way. Meriam-Webster's dictionary defines Change as, to make different in some particular way, to make radically different, to give a position, course or direction to, to replace with another, to undergo a modification. To shift ones means of conveyance, or to undergo transformation, transition, of substitution. When I compared that definition to life, I came to the conclusion that change is basically what life is about. Life is adapting to change, transition, and substitution. In life, we are constantly changing or adapting to situations and/or events that occur in life. Whether those events are good or bad, we have to choose to adapt the change that it may or may not cause. These changes invoke both good and bad emotions, depending on the situation. Sometimes we are able to change the situation but other times we are forced to change ourselves. As you read this book and complete these exercises, I want you to be mindful of the people and situations that force you to change self. This book was intended for those times, when you need an extra push to change yourself to adapt to the change in a person or situation.

You know when you are at the point where you are no longer able to change the situation, and are challenged to change yourself? I consider this the space where you become stuck. You do not know which way to go or where to turn. That is where this book comes to play. This book provides various exercises and coping skills so that your journey on life and change is a little less stressful and a little less emotional. Let's be honest, we all have those times of uncertainty or the times when our wellbeing is affected. So, my hope is that when you come into those life events that force you to change yourself, you will pick up this book and be able to twirl through those changes with a breeze. Happy reading and do not forget to GLOW!

The first exercise is for you to list below the times that you were forced to change yourself versus change the situation. Complete the exercise below by answering each question honestly. The point of this is for you to recognize your strengths and to see that if you have done it before you can do it again.

If I Did It Once, I Can Do It Again!

In this exercise, I give space and ask you to identify ten situations or life events from the past that forced you to change yourself. If you do not have ten that's OK, just complete what you can. I challenge you to pay attention to life events that cause you to change yourself versus changing the situations as you continue to live, because like I have stated life is full of changes. Some of the answers to these questions will also help you complete other exercises in this book.

Name a situation that you were forced to change yourself:

_____
_____
_____
_____

What helped me change myself:

_____
_____
_____
_____

What was not helpful:

_____
_____
_____
_____

Who was helpful:

_____
_____
_____
_____

Who was not helpful:

_____
_____
_____
_____

What was the end result (name only good things we are focusing on the positive vibes):

_____
_____
_____
_____

Name a situation that you were forced to change yourself:

_____
_____
_____
_____

What helped me change myself:

_____
_____
_____
_____

What was not helpful:

_____
_____
_____
_____

Who was helpful:

_____
_____
_____
_____

Who was not helpful:

_____
_____
_____
_____

What was the end result (name only good things we are focusing on the positive vibes):

_____
_____
_____
_____

Name a situation that you were forced to change yourself:

_____
_____
_____
_____

What helped me change myself:

_____
_____
_____
_____

What was not helpful:

_____
_____
_____
_____

Who was helpful:

_____
_____
_____
_____

Who was not helpful:

_____
_____
_____
_____

What was the end result (name only good things we are focusing on the positive vibes):

_____
_____
_____
_____

Name a situation that you were forced to change yourself:

_____
_____
_____
_____

What helped me change myself:

_____
_____
_____
_____

What was not helpful:

_____
_____
_____
_____

Who was helpful:

_____
_____
_____
_____

Who was not helpful:

_____
_____
_____

What was the end result (name only good things we are focusing on the positive vibes):

_____
_____
_____
_____

Name a situation that you were forced to change yourself:

_____
_____
_____

What helped me change myself:

_____
_____
_____

What was not helpful:

_____
_____
_____

Who was helpful:

_____
_____
_____

Who was not helpful:

_____
_____
_____

What was the end result (name only good things we are focusing on the positive vibes):

_____
_____
_____
_____

Name a situation that you were forced to change yourself:

_____
_____
_____
_____

What helped me change myself:

_____
_____
_____
_____

What was not helpful:

_____
_____
_____
_____

Who was helpful:

_____
_____
_____
_____

Who was not helpful:

_____
_____
_____

What was the end result (name only good things we are focusing on the positive vibes):

_____
_____
_____
_____

Name a situation that you were forced to change yourself:

_____
_____
_____
_____

What helped me change myself:

_____
_____
_____
_____

What was not helpful:

_____
_____
_____
_____

Who was helpful:

_____
_____
_____
_____

Who was not helpful:

_____
_____
_____
_____

What was the end result (name only good things we are focusing on the positive vibes):

_____
_____
_____
_____

Name a situation that you were forced to change yourself:

_____
_____
_____
_____

What helped me change myself:

_____
_____
_____
_____

What was not helpful:

_____
_____
_____
_____

Who was helpful:

_____
_____
_____
_____

Who was not helpful:

_____
_____
_____
_____

What was the end result (name only good things we are focusing on the positive vibes):

_____
_____
_____
_____

Name a situation that you were forced to change yourself:

_____
_____
_____

What helped me change myself:

_____
_____
_____

What was not helpful:

_____
_____
_____

Who was helpful:

_____
_____
_____

Who was not helpful:

_____
_____
_____

What was the end result (name only good things we are focusing on the positive vibes):

_____
_____
_____
_____

Name a situation that you were forced to change yourself:

_____
_____
_____
_____

What helped me change myself:

_____
_____
_____
_____

What was not helpful:

_____
_____
_____
_____

Who was helpful:

_____
_____
_____
_____

Who was not helpful:

_____
_____
_____

What was the end result (name only good things we are focusing on the positive vibes):

_____
_____
_____
_____

Notes and ides

"Each person deserves a day away in which no problems are confronted and no solutions searched for. Each of us needs to withdraw from the cares, which will not withdraw from us."
-Maya Angelou

Take a Break

First things first, when you find yourself about to give up and no longer able to breathe, think, eat, or move take a break. I believe that when you hit a rough spot in life and find yourself not able to tell the difference on whether you are coming or going, you need to take some time to yourself. I suggest taking seven days to reset your mind, body, and soul. Do not take no more than seven days, as taking more time may cause you to become stuck in your feelings for longer than necessary. During these seven days you can take a trip, stay home, or do whatever helps you get back to you as long as it helps you get back to YOU!

You are entitled to as many breaks as you need throughout life and you owe no one an explanation. As time go on you may even notice that you no longer need the full seven days to reset and might be able to reset off 2 days. Whatever the case maybe, remember that only you know when you need to take a break. And if you are unable to identify when you need a break don't fret there are exercises in this book to help you identify the signs.

Although there have been many times I should have taken a break in my life, I remember the very first time I actually took a break. I was working as an in-home therapist for a local agency and was going through a very tough break-up with an ex of five years. I was a total wreck. Some days I did not know if I was coming or going. I would cry myself to sleep at night and barely was getting any sleep. I would go to work and see my clients, but my mind was not into helping anyone at the time as I could not even help myself. I would be sitting in session thinking to myself, how am I going to make it? I cannot believe he just left me. Maybe I should call and try to work it out. What didn't I do? Why doesn't he want me?

Now imagine how I am supposed to help someone in such a fragile state. I thought I was failing my clients because I was emotionally going through what I thought was the worst time in my life. I would cancel appointments on days that it was really rough and to my surprise my clients did not have a second thought about the cancellation. They did not even realize that I was going through my own emotional battle. But I knew, so being the responsible person, I am, I resigned from my position. Yes, you read correctly; I just quit. I put in my two-week notice and met with each and every one of my clients to let them know they were going to be assigned to a new therapist. I even made introductions to the new therapists to ensure the transition was easy.

I know some of you are reading this and are in disbelief, but it was important for me to take that break because self-care and taking time outs are vital to your emotional wellbeing. And sometimes you cannot properly heal while wearing a superwoman/man cape. So, take a break when you need one or two but do not, I repeat do not repress your emotions and carry on like a robot.

My Notes& Ideas

Hint: use this space to list places you can go or things you can do when you need a break!

"It's OK if you fall down and lose your spark. Just make sure that when you get back up, you rise as the whole damn fire."

-Colette Werden

<u>*Getting Back To Me list*</u>

In the space below I want you to make a list of every goal, every idea, or anything you wanted to try or accomplish and have not thus far. The list does not have to be in any specific order just start where ever your mind takes you. Then when you come back from your break, look at this list and pick 1-2 things that you can start working on immediately.

For example: *If you wanted to get a bachelor's degree or finish that degree you started, start looking at schools and different ways to finish that degree. In doing this you are taking your mind and energy away from the situation at hand or the person who caused hurt and putting your mind and energy back into you!*

_____

_____
_____
_____
_____
_____
_____
_____
_____
_____
_____
_____
_____
_____
_____
_____
_____
_____
_____
_____
_____
_____
_____
_____
_____
_____
_____
_____
_____
_____

Notes and Ideas

My Getting Back To Me Daily List

You may or may not have noticed that there are certain things you need to do daily to remain at 100%. This plan helps you identify things you need to do daily to remain physically healthy, mentally healthy, emotionally healthy, and spiritually healthy. When you begin to feel off track, you probably neglected to do something on your daily maintenance list.

For Example: *Every morning when I wake up, I have a daily ritual. I first read my daily devotional; I turn on my gospel music and burn sage all while showering and getting dressed. Lastly, I continue to listen to gospel music on my way to work to start my day off on a good foot. Use the answers to the following questions to identify your daily maintenance and as a daily reminder.*

This is how I feel and look at 100% or how I would like to fell and look at 100%:

_____
_____
_____
_____
_____
_____
_____
_____

These are the things I need to do daily to be at a 100%:

_____
_____
_____
_____
_____
_____

These are the things I need to do weekly to be at 100%:

_____
_____
_____
_____
_____
_____
_____

<u>My Getting Back To Me List Continued</u>

These are the things I need to do monthly to be at a 100%:

_____

_____
_____
_____
_____
_____
_____

These are the things I need to do Periodically to make sure I'm at 100%:

_____

_____
_____
_____
_____
_____
_____

I can do these special things for myself to be at a 100%:

_____

_____
_____
_____
_____
_____
_____

Notes and Ideas

Recognizing My Triggers

These are the things that happen that cause an increase in my stress or emotions. If any of the following things should happen or occur, I will use the list in the following section to keep my stress and emotions from taking over.

List of my Triggers:

_____
_____
_____
_____
_____
_____
_____
_____
_____
_____

If any of my triggers occur, I will do the following:

_____
_____
_____
_____
_____
_____
_____
_____
_____
_____
_____
_____
_____
_____

*Now I know a few of you are looking at the word **Trigger** and giving it a side eye. You are probably saying to yourself right now, I do not have any triggers. I'm here to tell you we all have triggers; even me. I have certain things that really melt my butter or grind my gears. And these things may not be a big deal to someone else but to me they are a big deal. I say that because I need for you to understand what bothers you or stresses you out, may not bother or stress other people out. That does not mean that there is something wrong with you or them, it just means that everyone interprets a situation or occurrence differently then you. And guess what; it's OK because we are all human and God created us all differently.*

Some of my triggers are:

I do not like when people touch my stuff i.e. moving it without permission, eat my left-over food etc.

If you're moving something of mine, let me know. If you're going to eat my food, let me know. If you're going to use something of mine, let me know. Because I do not like going back looking for something and it is gone or having my mouth ready to eat my scrumptious left overs only to find that it is gone.

I do not like when people try to solve my problems when I do not ask for their help i.e. I vent to you about a situation and you go to the person in attempt to fix it before I can fix the problem. I'm grown I can fix my own problems.

I do not like being lied to or liars. I consider myself an easy-going person and would rather be hurt by the truth versus a lie.

And lastly when any of the above occurs, I usually call my mother because she is always the voice of reason for me. She is one person I can trust, and I know she will never just tell my business. I also will let the person who did any of the above know in the kindest way possible that I do not like that they lied, moved my stuff, or tried to solve my problem. I let them know it bothers me and explain that I rather they not do it from this point forward.

Notes and Ideas

"The truth is, unless you let go, unless you forgive yourself, unless you forgive the situation, unless you realize that the situation is over, you cannot move forward."
-Steve Maraboli

Forgiving or Letting Go!

Forgiveness starts with self. You must first learn how to forgive yourself before you can forgive anyone else. The process of forgiveness is all about you letting go of the hurt so you can become a better you.

Learning to forgive or letting go of a person, situations, or object is hard for all of us. I get it, sometimes holding on to the hurt is comfort or it validates how you feel in some sort of strange way. But I'm here to tell you that forgiving or letting go is 100% all for your betterment. When you learn to forgive someone who did you wrong or let go of a situation that did not work in your favor, you excel to higher heights. You feel lighter and your days become shorter and easier. I know it's hard to forgive someone or something that has caused you hurt and even harder to forgive yourself, so I've provided an exercise that will help you learn to forgive and let go for the hard days. Practice makes perfect and if you practice this exercise, you will find it will make you feel lighter each day, each week, and each month and getting over things will become a second nature.

Letting Go!

We have all heard the phrase "Girl just let that go" or "Don't worry about it, you will get over it soon." But in all actuality, letting go or not worrying about it is easier said than done. In therapy, we have an exercise to help you get over grief, anger, or depression. You write a letter to the person or about the situation that caused you grief, depression or anger, read it out loud, then burn it to symbolize your process of "letting go" or "getting over" the whole ordeal. I want to introduce to you the "Letting go jar" or for lack of better words the "Fuck it jar" "Fuck that Jar." If you have a jar or tin lying around, I want to challenge you to write down all the things, people, places, or situations that piss you off or put you in a bad mood throughout the day or week and put them in the jar. At the end of the week I want you to burn them all. This exercise will help you practice letting things go. You will eventually realize that letting things go will become easier in the days, weeks, and months to come.

As I stated before, forgiveness starts with self. I honestly battle with this one because I'm harder on myself than anyone else. Like most people, I hold myself to a high standard so when I fail, or things did not work out the way I want them to work out, I really take things hard and personal. Over the years I have learned to be a lot easier on myself. I remember when I first learned I was pregnant with my daughter. I was in my last year of undergrad and felt as if I failed. I had made it through the military and through my entire life of having sex without any mishaps. I could not believe I was so irresponsible. I had unprotected sex, and now I'm pregnant. What am I going to do? How will I raise a child? Will I be able to finish school? These were the question running through my twenty-four-year-old brain. Like seriously out of all the men I could have gotten pregnant by I get pregnant by the one who I know for a fact was not going to be able to support me. I think I went through my whole first trimester in a state of shock and depression. I isolated myself from family and friends because I was embarrassed. I was suppose to get through these milestones kid free, so I thought. But it wasn't until I sat down with the dean of my department that I learned how important it was to forgive myself and keep pushing forward.

One day I was in her office crying of course because you know how emotional us women are when we are pregnant. And she said to me "what are you going to do," because at this time I was still contemplating on keeping my daughter or having an abortion. She explained to me it was my choice and that it's harder for me to do what others believe I should do versus doing what I want to do. She explained to me that if I chose to get an abortion to make my family and mother happy, I would be miserable because keeping my child and going the road frequently traveled was way harder for me versus going the road less traveled. It was right there and then I learned to forgive myself. I'm not perfect and I make mistakes. I forgave myself for getting pregnant by someone I knew could not be there for me and my child in the long run. I accepted the fact that I did not want to have an abortion and decided/accepted the fact that I would be a single parent. I also took a valuable lesson that day; when faced with a choice, always go with the hardest choice or the choice few would choose because that is usually the best choice for you. And look at me I'm glowing and I'm living as a single mother and all. I'm still knocking each goal I set for myself, out the park. You too, can learn to forgive yourself and others and still accomplish everything you want to accomplish.

Notes and ideas

"Life is short don't waste it with negative people who don't appreciate you. Keep them in your heart but keep them out your life."

-Anonymous

List of Positive, Negative, and Neutral People

*When writing this list, I do not want you to think of people that have negative or positive energy. I want you to think of people who respond to your idea, your goals, or what you have to say in a negative or positive way. The people on your positive list should be people who when you share something with them they have a positive response, something good or hopeful to say. The people on your negative list are the ones who have something negative to say or something bad to say about your ideas or goals. Now the neutral people are the people when you tell them about your goals or ideas they have NOTHING to say or will just respond "oh OK." The negative and neutral list you should never use when you want to vent or have something exciting to share because they do not add value to your life or encourage you do go forward or do better. I'm not saying to forget them all together, but I am saying do not go to them for encouragement or support. You already know that you will not find the response you want so why continue to get bit by the same dog twice as my grandmother would say. (**hint**: you can use the people from your list you identified as the person who you considered helpful you to change yourself)*

Positive list	Negative List	Neutral List

Now this list is vital! People often think that they cannot put family, friends or parents on their negative list. I am here to tell you that yes, your friends, your family, and even your parents can be negative Nancy's. Yes, some people do not have encouraging parents, some parents just do not possess the quality of encouragement when it comes down to their children. If you have parents that are always finding fault in something you do, then place them on your negative list. The same rules apply to friends and family. And guess what, this is OK. There is nothing wrong with having family and friends that behave in the above manner. We have to realize everyone has strong points and some peoples are just not very strong at being supportive or encouraging others to reach higher heights, their strengths maybe in other areas. If you find that you do not have anyone to place on your positive list for encouragement, then seek the help you need in a therapist. I can be reached via e-mail anyeaanderson@gmail.com and I'm available for virtual sessions. If you want to find a therapist in your area you can also utilize Psychology Today website and Therapy for Black Girls directory for therapist in your area. The benefits of having a therapist are wonderful plus they offer a non-bias opinion on real life issues.

"Grief is like the ocean; it comes on waves ebbing and flowing. Sometimes the water is calm, and sometimes it is overwhelming. All we can do is learn to swim."
-Vicki Harrison

Grief/ Separation and Loss

When we think of grief, we automatically attach it to the death of someone we love. But I'm here to tell you we can feel grief in many situations; divorce, relationships endings, break ups, not meeting our goals, or not meeting our accomplishments. Grief can slow you down and prohibit your progress and with anything in life, it is a process to learn to live without what your heart was hoping to last forever or even not living up to your full potential. But I am here to tell you that life will continue to go on you will find your happily ever after no matter what situation you are grieving. Sometimes separation brings elevation. During this time of grieving, you are transitioning. You are learning to adapt and adjust to the situation or person no longer being in your life. So, I have provided an exercise to help you grieve properly so you can be the best you can be. Remember we are making lemonade out of all lemons.

The Five Stages of Grief

Elizabeth Kubler-Ross developed what we call the five stages of grief; Denial, Anger, Bargaining, Depression, and Acceptance. You may go through all five stages or you may only go through two or three. Theses stages do not occur in any specific order and it is likely that you may re-visit a couple of stages while you are going through your grieving process or skip a few.

Denial- this is the stage when you fail to acknowledge the event. You may opt out of addressing it by going on a trip or taking a break. Taking a temporary break is healthy in most cases, but it becomes unhealthy when you totally ignore your emotions and never coming back from the break to face reality or continue with your day to day routines. This is the stage when you receive the initial shock of realizing you lost someone. Whether it be a death of a family member, the deal that you hope to go through or a break-up/divorce.

Denial is the initial stage you become numb or even go into shock! This is where you may just mentally and physically check out. You may take your break during this stage, isolate yourself from everyone, or even ignore the situation and pretend it never happened. But this is the stage that sets the catalyst for how much you can take and what you can handle. This stage is unconsciously making you stronger.

Anger- This is where you may lash out at anyone or anything that is related to the lost. Whether it be a doctor who was unable to save your loved one, your significant other who you blame for the demise of the relationship, the other woman/man, or the company/person of the contract or job that did not work out.

Anger is the stage that you begin to question Why me? Or even question God or whatever your higher power maybe. And if it's a break-up/ divorce you may ask Why her? What didn't I do right? You may even approach that person full of rage and give them a piece of your mind. But, there is no explanation to why or none that will be a reasonable explanation for your current pain. The feeling of anger provides you with a connection to what you have lost and is normal.

Bargaining- This is when you try to rationalize the loss. If only I would have cooked more, cleaned more, or I could have done this instead of that. This is the stage where you try to figure out what you could have done to avoid the inevitable from occurring.

Bargaining is the stage where you play the blame game. And guess what, you put all the blame on yourself. You "If only" yourself to death in this stage. You feel guilty in this stage and think of all the things you could have done to prevent the situation from occurring. But in all honesty there is nothing you could have done to prevent the situation because what happened is usually out of your control.

Depression-There are two types of depression we go through when we are grieving. We seek reassurance from friends and relatives, we look for encouraging words and worry about the loss or what it will cost by taking the loss. The second type is isolation. We separate ourselves from any and everyone and go through the pain of the loss alone. Feelings of depression are also normal when you suffer a loss of any kind and it DOES NOT MEAN YOU SUFFER FROM A

MENTAL ILLNESS. We all suffer from some form of depression or down stage when we suffer a loss.

Depression is that can't eat, can't sleep, can't breathe stage. You may find yourself wondering and questioning can life go on? And you may find that the things you use to enjoy doing you no longer enjoy doing. In this stage your family and friends may even view you as a negative Nancy. But do not worry it is perfectly normal, to not experience some type of depression after a lost or death is UNSUAL!

Acceptance- This is the stage where a person is perceived to be "alright" or "OK." But to be honest this is the stage where you begin to accept reality that you took a LOSS! You begin to live again and feel alive in this stage. And yes, there will be times when you re-visit the what ifs or the possibility/thoughts of how what you have loss did not work out or how your "happily ever after" did not end happily. But in this stage you are able to re-focus and get back to living.

Acceptance is the stage where you will find yourself attempting to complete some of those things on your GETTING BACK TO ME LIST! This is the stage where looking at pictures of your loved ones or seeing that ex is with someone else does not bother you, it no longer cause you pain.

Reflecting

Because there maybe a few times or situations in life where you may need to reflect I have included several spaces for the future.

What did this person or situation bring to your life? *Was it financial gain? Was it stress? Was it joy?*

_____

_____

_____

How did this person or situation make you feel? *Did it make you feel positive or negative? Did it bring out the best in you or the worst in you?*

_____

_____

_____

How did the environment feel when you were around the person or in the situation? *Did it encourage or discourage you? Did it breathe life into you or wreak havoc on your life?*

_____

_____

_____

Was this person or situation beneficial to your goals? *Did it encourage you to reach further or get in the way? Did it cause you to go harder or was it just in the way or you going further?*

_____

_____

_____

Without this person or situation in your life will you no longer be able to live? *Will you no longer be able to breathe? Will you lose a limb? Will it cause bodily harm?*

_____

_____

_____

What did this person or situation bring to your life? *Was it financial gain? Was it stress? Was it joy?*

_____
_____
_____

How did this person or situation make you feel? *Did it make you feel positive or negative? Did it bring out the best in you or the worst in you?*

_____
_____
_____

How did the environment feel when you were around the person or in the situation? *Did it encourage or discourage you? Did it breathe life into you or wreak havoc on your life?*

_____
_____
_____

Was this person or situation beneficial to your goals? *Did it encourage you to reach further or get in the way? Did it cause you to go harder or was it just in the way or you going further?*

_____
_____
_____

Without this person or situation in your life will you no longer be able to live? *Will you no longer be able to breathe? Will you use a limb? Will it cause bodily harm?*

_____
_____
_____

What did this person or situation bring to your life? *Was it financial gain? Was it stress? Was it joy?*

_____
_____
_____

How did this person or situation make you feel? *Did it make you feel positive or negative? Did it bring out the best in you or the worst in you?*

_____
_____
_____

How did the environment feel when you were around the person or in the situation? *Did it encourage or discourage you? Did it breathe life into you or wreak havoc on your life?*

_____
_____
_____

Was this person or situation beneficial to your goals? *Did it encourage you to reach further or get in the way? Did it cause you to go harder or was it just in the way or you going further?*

_____
_____
_____

Without this person or situation in your life will you no longer be able to live? *Will you no longer be able to breathe? Will you use a limb? Will it cause bodily harm?*

_____
_____
_____

What did this person or situation bring to your life? *Was it financial gain? Was it stress? Was it joy?*

_____

_____

_____

How did this person or situation make you feel? *Did it make you feel positive or negative? Did it bring out the best in you or the worst in you?*

_____

_____

_____

How did the environment feel when you were around the person or in the situation? *Did it encourage or discourage you? Did it breathe life into you or wreak havoc on your life?*

_____

_____

_____

Was this person or situation beneficial to your goals? *Did it encourage you to reach further or get in the way? Did it cause you to go harder or was it just in the way or you going further?*

_____

_____

_____

Without this person or situation in your life will you no longer be able to live? *Will you no longer be able to breathe? Will you use a limb? Will it cause bodily harm?*

_____

_____

_____

What did this person or situation bring to your life? *Was it financial gain? Was it stress? Was it joy?*

_____

_____

_____

How did this person or situation make you feel? *Did it make you feel positive or negative? Did it bring out the best in you or the worst in you?*

_____

_____

_____

How did the environment feel when you were around the person or in the situation? *Did it encourage or discourage you? Did it breathe life into you or wreak havoc on your life?*

_____

_____

_____

Was this person or situation beneficial to your goals? *Did it encourage you to reach further or get in the way? Did it cause you to go harder or was it just in the way or you going further?*

_____

_____

_____

Without this person or situation in your life will you no longer be able to live? *Will you no longer be able to breathe? Will you use a limb? Will it cause bodily harm?*

_____

_____

_____

What did this person or situation bring to your life? *Was it financial gain? Was it stress? Was it joy?*

_____
_____
_____

How did this person or situation make you feel? *Did it make you feel positive or negative? Did it bring out the best in you or the worst in you?*

_____
_____
_____

How did the environment feel when you were around the person or in the situation? *Did it encourage or discourage you? Did it breathe life into you or wreak havoc on your life?*

_____
_____
_____

Was this person or situation beneficial to your goals? *Did it encourage you to reach further or get in the way? Did it cause you to go harder or was it just in the way or you going further?*

_____
_____
_____

Without this person or situation in your life will you no longer be able to live? *Will you no longer be able to breathe? Will you use a limb? Will it cause bodily harm?*

_____
_____
_____

What did this person or situation bring to your life? *Was it financial gain? Was it stress? Was it joy?*

_____
_____
_____

How did this person or situation make you feel? *Did it make you feel positive or negative? Did it bring out the best in you or the worst in you?*

_____
_____
_____

How did the environment feel when you were around the person or in the situation? *Did it encourage or discourage you? Did it breathe life into you or wreak havoc on your life?*

_____
_____
_____

Was this person or situation beneficial to your goals? *Did it encourage you to reach further or get in the way? Did it cause you to go harder or was it just in the way or you going further?*

_____
_____
_____

Without this person or situation in your life will you no longer be able to live? *Will you no longer be able to breathe? Will you use a limb? Will it cause bodily harm?*

_____
_____
_____

What did this person or situation bring to your life? *Was it financial gain? Was it stress? Was it joy?*

_____

_____

_____

How did this person or situation make you feel? *Did it make you feel positive or negative? Did it bring out the best in you or the worst in you?*

_____

_____

_____

How did the environment feel when you were around the person or in the situation? *Did it encourage or discourage you? Did it breathe life into you or wreak havoc on your life?*

_____

_____

_____

Was this person or situation beneficial to your goals? *Did it encourage you to reach further or get in the way? Did it cause you to go harder or was it just in the way or you going further?*

_____

_____

_____

Without this person or situation in your life will you no longer be able to live? *Will you no longer be able to breathe? Will you use a limb? Will it cause bodily harm?*

_____

_____

_____

What did this person or situation bring to your life? *Was it financial gain? Was it stress? Was it joy?*

_____
_____
_____

How did this person or situation make you feel? *Did it make you feel positive or negative? Did it bring out the best in you or the worst in you?*

_____
_____
_____

How did the environment feel when you were around the person or in the situation? *Did it encourage or discourage you? Did it breathe life into you or wreak havoc on your life?*

_____
_____
_____

Was this person or situation beneficial to your goals? *Did it encourage you to reach further or get in the way? Did it cause you to go harder or was it just in the way or you going further?*

_____
_____
_____

Without this person or situation in your life will you no longer be able to live? *Will you no longer be able to breathe? Will you use a limb? Will it cause bodily harm?*

_____
_____
_____

What did this person or situation bring to your life? *Was it financial gain? Was it stress? Was it joy?*

_____

_____

_____

How did this person or situation make you feel? *Did it make you feel positive or negative? Did it bring out the best in you or the worst in you?*

_____

_____

_____

How did the environment feel when you were around the person or in the situation? *Did it encourage or discourage you? Did it breathe life into you or wreak havoc on your life?*

_____

_____

_____

Was this person or situation beneficial to your goals? *Did it encourage you to reach further or get in the way? Did it cause you to go harder or was it just in the way or you going further?*

_____

_____

_____

Without this person or situation in your life will you no longer be able to live? *Will you no longer be able to breathe? Will you use a limb? Will it cause bodily harm?*

_____

_____

_____

What did this person or situation bring to your life? *Was it financial gain? Was it stress? Was it joy?*

_____
_____
_____

How did this person or situation make you feel? *Did it make you feel positive or negative? Did it bring out the best in you or the worst in you?*

_____
_____
_____

How did the environment feel when you were around the person or in the situation? *Did it encourage or discourage you? Did it breathe life into you or wreak havoc on your life?*

_____
_____
_____

Was this person or situation beneficial to your goals? *Did it encourage you to reach further or get in the way? Did it cause you to go harder or was it just in the way or you going further?*

_____
_____
_____

Without this person or situation in your life will you no longer be able to live? *Will you no longer be able to breathe? Will you use a limb? Will it cause bodily harm?*

_____
_____
_____

There are two major losses I took in life that has really took a toll on my life. One was a physical loss; the death of my pop-pop and the other was the ending of a relationship. Both caused major hurt and pain in my life but my recovery from both were very different.

The death of my pop-pop, who technically was my great-uncle, was very painful. I believe it was painful because he died in the house that I was living in at the time. I remember the day like it was yesterday. I was leaving for work and it was only me, my daughter who was an infant at the time, and my pop-pop in the home that morning. I came down the steps and noticed that the bathroom door was closed. I said, "see you later pop-pop." I did not get a response and thought nothing of it at the time. I dropped my daughter off at daycare and go on to work. About an hour or so I get a call from my mother saying that my Aunt found my pop-pop in the bathroom on the floor unresponsive and he did not make it. I dropped to me knees at work and cried my eyes out. I felt guilty because in my mind, I am thinking I should have knocked on the door, I should have gone into the bathroom when I did not get a response, I should not have just left. What If I could have saved my pop-pop? I had a million-what if's running through my head. I do not think I ate or spoke to anyone for like a day or two. My mother came to me and said, "now Anyea, you must get up. You have to take care of your daughter. Pop-pop would not want you to be sitting here not talking or not eating." You see my pop-pop was one of my biggest supporters; I could do no wrong in his eyes. When I got pregnant with my daughter, my mother was very disappointed but my pop-pop said, "well come live with me and your Aunt." I did exactly that. I moved in with my pop-pop and him and my Aunt supported me my entire pregnancy and senior year in undergrad. My pop-pop even was there to pick me up bright and early from the hospital when it was time for me to be discharged after giving birth. At the time he was supporting me, he never told me he was battling cancer. He remained as his happy go lucky self. You know how I got through the pain of losing my pop-pop? I remembered all the good times. All the track meets, basketball games, cheerleading events he attended over the years and short time he was with me to help me out with my daughter. I have many memories with my pop-pop and it was through those memories I was able to push through and keep going.

Now the second one was way harder to get over. Mainly because it was the longest and first real relationship I had been in my entire life. When my ex and I broke up after five years, I was devastated. I could not sleep; I could not eat, or even function correctly for months. I thought he was going to be my forever. I was sadly mistaken. And yes, this is the same guy that had me take my first break. I did a lot of reflecting after we went our separate ways and started putting all the energy I once put into trying to make our relationship work back into myself. It was a much longer process of recovery getting over the break-up. I think it took me about a year to fully recover. I know a lot of you guys are reading a year? That is a long time. But I did not walk around in a depressed mood for a year. I just went through the five stages of grief that whole year. The majority of the time I went from denial, depression, acceptance, and rationalizing stage until I finally just accepted that we were no longer together and there was no coming back. That year I did a lot of praying, a lot of journaling, and putting a lot of energy into the things on my Get Back to me List. Reflecting on that time, I believe it was vital for who I am today. That break-up made me stronger and wiser. I'm so thankful for the pain now because I wouldn't have even written this book if it was not for the pain of that break-up. The break-up gave me a new life.

Notes and Ideas

No matter how you feel, Get Up, Dress Up, Show Up, And Never Give Up."

-Anonymous

You Don't Look Like What You Been Through

I remember going through the roughest break-up of my life. I was literally dying inside. I felt like the world as I knew it was being pulled from under my feet and at any moment, I was going to fall flat on my face. I began to separate myself from my friends and would decline every invitation for dinner or girls night out. One week, I decided that this was the week I was going out and enjoy spending time with my girlfriends. I did what most of us women do to ensure you are on point; nails, hair, make-up, etc. While at dinner with my friends, I decided to disclose what I had been going through and give my friends the "tea." I will never forget what one of my friends said to me that night after disclosing what I have been dealing with for months. "Well you don't look like what you been going through. I couldn't even tell." At that moment I realized "I don't look like what I've been through." Yes, I had countless sleepless nights and nights I literally cried myself to sleep but each day I woke up, I got dressed and gave the day all I had.

In life we will go through moments, times, and situations where you feel you are at your worst. But you must always remember that even at your worst you must remain "your best" to the public eye. Your pain and hurt is not for everyone and you should never let it show on the outside. I'm not suggesting that you pretend that everything is "ok" but what I am suggesting is that you continue to do your daily maintenance or maintain your outward appearance. Do not, I repeat do not show up to work every day looking like you just rolled out of bed. You have to have the mindset that *I got control of this situation; this situation does not have control over me.* This can be as simple as not throwing your hair in a ponytail and continuing to style your hair in the morning. Do whatever helps to make you look good, because if you look good it helps you feel good. If you are unable to pinpoint what or how you can make yourself look good, so you can feel good daily, try writing a list that you can look at for helpful reminders.

Things that I can do that will help me look and feel good daily

I can get up and do my hair daily.
I can get up and do my make-up daily.
I can continue to dress well daily.

Notes and Ideas

"No is a complete sentence. It does not require an explanation to follow. You can truly answer someone's request with a simple No."

-Sharon E. Riley

Learning to say "No"

Sometimes saying "no" comes easy and sometimes it doesn't. In life, we may have to say "no" numerous times to people we love dearly but are unable to or do not know how to say "no." This is exercise is solely for the purpose of when you run into the hard times of you being unable to say "no." I actually have done a group entitled, _Refusal Skills,_ with some of my clients on how to say "no" to help them get comfortable with telling someone they love or someone they consider important "no." These are just tips and things to assist you in saying "no" when that time comes.

Refusal Skills

1. Give a reason for refusal (When saying no, also state a reason, BE HONEST) Example: No, because if I pay your electricity bill this month how will you pay it next month

2. Use body language to reinforce what you say (Body language can strengthen or weaken your message) Example: Do not be meek sweating and pacing be able to look the person in the eye and say "no".

3. Show concern for others (Express your concerns for those trying to persuade you) Example: No, because I will not because you need to have a permit or licenses to do that and if you do not you may get a fine or jail time. I do not think jail, or a fine is something you need at this time.

4. Provide alternatives (No let's go to the movies) Example: No, I think you should finish what you started then move on to the next step

5. Take definite action (Remove yourself from the situation) Example: This is when you chose to just leave or utilize the block feature on your phone or e-mail

Notes and Ideas

Notes and ideas continued

Learning to say No is hard for all of us. I do not have a specific situation to where I said No to someone or situation, but I know all too well how it feels to have to say no to family and friends that you want to say Yes to. I have a very bad habit of over extending myself especially, to family. I'm the type of person that if family needs me whether blood or not, I'm there. Once I moved to Atlanta, I was living in a house with more than enough room that if a family member called me and said, "I'm moving to Atlanta or need a place to stay"; my door was wide open. At one point, I had family living with me and thought that we were helping each other. But in reality, I was over exerting myself. I learned that I cannot help or pour from an empty cup. I learned that in order for me to be able to help family, I have to have a cup that runneth over and cannot pour from and empty cup. I realized that I cannot help people if I am not able to help myself. So, at one point you would find multiple family members living with me until they can get on their feet to get their own place to live. But today I understand the importance of having peace and not over exerting myself. I am a single mother that does not receive any help from her child's father and I would rather do bad by myself versus having an audience to see me do bad. So, I made a choice to not allow anyone to stay with me or provide my assistance or help to family that I cannot afford to not get back; that includes money or housing. So today, no you cannot stay with me and no you cannot borrow or get $20 from me if I cannot stand to not live without the $20 or money to help pay for bills. It may seem harsh, but it is reality. I learned that people believe you have all the money in the word because you have a certain type of job or certain amount of education. But what they do not realize is how much money or bills you have, they never take in accountability that it really cost to be a boss. And for that reason, if I am not making enough money to take on the extra responsibility of someone else, it must be a NO for me from here on out. So, no I cannot give you any money or a place to stay because all my funds are tied up in my bills and things I need to raise my daughter ALONE! Iyanla Vanzant said it best you cannot pour from an empty cup, it's easier to pour when your cup runneth over.

"You gain strength, courage, and confidence by every experience in which you really stop to look fear in the face. You are able to say to yourself, 'I lived through this horror. I can take the next thing that comes along.'"

-Eleanor Roosevelt

Fear

In therapy, we use two acronyms for F.E.A.R; Forget Everything and Run or Face Everything and Rise; the one you chose is solely your choice. The most common emotion fear brings is anxiety. You are not able to make a rational decision, you procrastinate on making the decision, you begin to sweat or you're unable to concentrate. My suggestion to getting over what you fear is to face everything and rise. And yes, I know this is a hard task for all of us, so I provided an exercise to help assist you with what you fear the most. In this exercise, I want you to make a list of all the things you fear. Starting with the thing you fear the least and ending with the thing you fear the most. After making the list, I need you to write down the steps to how you can conquer each fear on the list. Then you need to take action. Lastly you need to list what it looks like when you have faced each fear on your list.

I remember going through a hard time dealing with being pregnant in my senior year of undergrad. I feared that I would not graduate with my degree and was in my department heads office crying. I will always remember what she said to me. "It is harder for you to do what others think you should do versus what you think you should do," meaning that I needed to do what came easiest for me versus what people were saying could or should happen. And guess what? I decided to do what my heart was set on and have my daughter and finish my senior year. To my surprise I was able to complete undergrad as a double major and I graduated three weeks after having my daughter. I did not let fear of not being able to complete my last year due to my pregnancy hold me back. If I did, I would not be writing this book or even hold my master's degree. You see, I Faced Everything and Rose.

List of things I Fear

Steps I can take to face my fears

_____

_____
_____
_____
_____
_____
_____
_____
_____
_____
_____
_____
_____
_____
_____
_____
_____
_____
_____
_____
_____
_____
_____
_____
_____
_____
_____
_____
_____
_____
_____
_____
_____
_____
_____
_____
_____
_____
_____
_____
_____
_____
_____
_____
_____
_____

How I know that I have faced my fears

I get it we all have fears, but it is what we do with those fears that really count. And like you, I have fears too. My biggest fear is failing; I never want to fail at things I start. This fear of failure has caused me to delay or not start projects a lot of times. But I learned to realize that if I never start, I never give myself the option to succeed or to fail. So, I decided at the start of 2017 that no matter if I succeed or fail, I would see my ideas through. For me failure is not an option. I believe in my little mind that everything I set out to do should be successful. Realistically that is not real because with success there is always some degree of failure. So now I try to think positively and not even bring the energy or thought of failure to mind when starting new projects. I go into the project with the mindset that it may blow the first time but then again it may not. I mentally prepare myself that things may not work out as plan. This way IF I fail and do not get the reaction from the public as I expected, I'm not that hard on myself. I also decided to give myself credit for just taking the initiative, seeing things through and taking the first step. Because being a single mother, working various jobs, and trying to get my business off the ground is a big accomplishment. There are some people who never go after their dreams or let their current financial situation prohibit them from making that first step. And here I am making them steps, moving forward, and believing in myself. So, no matter whether it's a hit or if it's a bust, I'm just happy now that I had the courage to do and not just think. If your feeling like this, it is OK just remember it takes a lot of courage to step out on faith and for that you should be proud of yourself.

Another fear I have that I have now faced was relocating to Atlanta, Georgia. Baby you could not get me to move from Trenton, New Jersey, me leave my mom and all my support. Now I knew in my heart I wanted to relocate here but I had it all planned out I would work at my demanding job for three more years, finish my graduate degree, save as much money as I could, and wait for my child to get a little older so it would be less strenuous. Well honey I did not follow that plan at all. I moved to Atlanta without my graduate degree, with little to no savings, and my daughter was just starting kindergarten. It was rough on me because I had never felt so alone, mainly I did not have my mother, my aunts, my grandma, or my brothers around to help me out. It is hard being a single mother trying to work, not having a baby sitter, trying to pick your child up on time so you will not get a late fee, and just being alone (yes, I had to say that again). But I'm glad I did it, yes, I'm glad because it forced me to grow up, now I have been grown for a long time but being on my own here in Atlanta, GA has really forced me to grow up. It has taught me a lot about being responsible. I will be the first to tell you I am spoiled yes, my mother spoils me to death, she never wants to see me face hard times. But I have learned that the hard times are the times that make you boss up and really proves the difference from the weak and the strong. I appreciate my success a little more, I appreciate that I earned my graduate degree a little more, and I appreciate the employments that I have been able to acquire because no one knew who I was it was all my interview and my resume. These relationships I'm building here in this city is solely off who I am as a person not who daughter, sister, or cousin I am. Yes, knowing people here has gotten me through some doors but if I do not have some substance I will just be so and so cousin. And yes, I have support and help here my cousins Aiesha, Erica, Tisha, Radiyah, Nakoreya, Narie, Big Korey, Cheryl and Nakia help me out a lot with my daughter from babysitting, pick-ups, and Cheryl my personal handy man lol. But having my mother or father here is just different for me. All and all I'm glad I moved to Atlanta and forever grateful for the love and support that I receive from my family because on days I do not believe in myself they believe in me they push me. And if they do not know they are the ones to push me to face my fears and not to stay complacent. Its because of my family and friend in this city I chose to BOSS UP!

"I'm Courageous enough to know I can Accomplish great things. I'm Humble enough to know when to ask for help."

-Katrina Mayer

Asking For Help????

In life, we all have to ask for help at some point even when we do not want to ask for help. When we are contemplating on who to ask or if we should ask, we begin to have thoughts or feeling like we will be a burden if we ask. There is no real way to get around this feeling, but you need to understand when you ask someone their only reply can be "no" or "yes."

You have to mentally prepare yourself that not everyone is willing or able to help you when you need the help. And understand that when a person says "no" it does not always mean they are hating; they just may not have the means or the ability to help you at that moment. So, if you need the help, ask and if you get a yes that's great and if you get a "no," all that means is NEXT OPTION. You cannot let a "no" deter you from going further or hold you back from trying to accomplish your goals or getting on with your life. And remember asking for help does not automatically make you a burden because remember, "those that mind don't matter and those that matter don't mind."

What we need to do before we ask for help is evaluate and recognize why asking for help is so hard. Did you have a negative experience in the past when you asked for help? Some negative experiences may look like this:

- You felt embarrassed after you asked for help
- The person you asked for help said "yes" but then later on threw the fact that they helped you, in your face
- The person helped you and then told your "business"
- The person helped you but ridiculed or talked down to you about needing their help in the first place
- When you accepted help it put you in a worse position than you were before

Above are just some examples and your negative experience in asking may look different. Below list some negative experiences you can attach with asking for help:

1. _____
2. _____
3. _____
4. _____
5. _____
6. _____
7. _____
8. _____
9. _____
10. _____

Now I want you to identify the people or person who you asked for help in the above situations or helped caused the above situation to occur below. THESE ARE THE PEOPLE YOU DO NOT ASK FOR HELP!

1._____
2._____
3._____
4._____
5._____
6._____
7._____
8._____
9._____
10._____

You may ask what was the purpose of doing the above? This helped you eliminate people, so you can identify who you CAN ask for help. Now don't feel guilty about who you place on the list above; the list holds no bias. You may find family members, parents, spouses, or even childhood friends. It is what it is like my grandmother always tell me "Never get bit by the same dog twice," meaning never put yourself in an uncomfortable situation twice if it's avoidable.

Who Can Help?

Below is a list you can use to help you identify; What you need help with? Who can help? What they can help with? When they can help you? And Where they can help you?

What I am specifically asking for is:_____
Who can help: _____
When can they help: _____
Where can they help: _____

What I am specifically asking for is:_____
Who can help: _____
When can they help: _____
Where can they help: _____

What I am specifically asking for is:_____
Who can help: _____
When can they help: _____
Where can they help: _____

What I am specifically asking for is:_____
Who can help: _____
When can they help: _____
Where can they help: _____

What I am specifically asking for is:_____
Who can help: _____
When can they help: _____
Where can they help: _____

What I am specifically asking for is:_____

Who can help: _____

When can they help: _____

Where can they help: _____

Remember to show appreciation a Thank you goes a long way and don't be afraid to ask for help when needed again.

Asking for help is something I battle with still to this day. I have to be completely honest, I do not like asking for help or rather I'm selective on who I ask. For so many years I was used to going to the same people for help; my mom, my dad, my brothers, certain cousins, particular aunts, and my godmother. I just didn't have the need to ask anyone else. But when I relocated to Atlanta, GA, I had none of those people here with me to ask for help. And after a while being or trying to be super woman wore me down. So, in turn I stared compiling a list of relatives and friends that I did not mind asking for help when I needed help. The list is not long but it's long enough to address my needs when I need the help. Accepting the fact that the only way I was going to be able to make it here in Atlanta, GA on my own was to accept help from others was not an easy battle for me. I moved here in 2012 and I am truly just getting comfortable with asking for help and it is 2018. And no, every time I call the people on my list are not always able to help me, but I have learned not to feel beat up inside and just move on to the next person. I have come to the realization that these people on my list have lives too and they are not sitting around waiting on me to call and tell them I need help with something or ask them can they help me with something. I have learned to adjust and adapt and if they cannot help me, I just will figure a way out, but what I will not do is start a pity party because that just causes more harm than good.

Notes & Ideas

"You control your future, your destiny. What you think about comes about. By recording your dreams and goals on paper, you set in motion the process of becoming the person you most want to be. Put your future in good hands, your own."
-Mark Victor Hansen

Goal Setting!!!!

Now setting a goal is way more than just writing something down on a piece of paper and having the thought that you will accomplish the goal. To actually accomplish a goal, you will have to make certain steps to make the goal attainable. When setting a goal, you must always remember to set SMART (Specific, Measurable, Attainable, Realistic, and Timely) goals.

You want to make your goals:

Specific- clear to anyone that can read or understand as well as well thought. In four years I will be walking across that stage with my bachelor's degree.

Measurable- Being able to tell when yourself that you have achieved the goal and make sure that it is actually an attainable goal for YOU. Do you have an idea of what it looks like when the goal is accomplished? How can you tell your goal was accomplished?

Attainable- Make sure this is a goal you can reach or that it is with-in your reach. Do not say by next month I am gone to have my cosmetology license and you are not in cosmetology school.

Realistic- That you yourself have the resources and information you need to reach your goal. Resources are not limited to just things you have yourself, it can include people you know or agencies/ companies that are familiar with who you are.

Timely- Give yourself a realistic time frame to achieve your goal. Do not give yourself a month to make 50K if you know you are not capable of making 50K in a month. Do not put that type of pressure on yourself; it causes more harm than good.

So many of us fail at accomplish our goals because we are not making SMART goals. As well as we do not think our steps out or write steps on how we plan to achieve our goals. I have included a monthly goal planner for you to use. You can use this goal planner however you see fit. But I suggest you take things off your 'Getting Back To Me' list and place them as monthly goals to get you started. Then write out steps and people that with-in your circle (positive people) who can help you reach that goal, if you need help. HAPPY GOAL SETTING, GLOW UP!

**Monthly Goal Planner**

**January**

My Goal for this month is:

_____
_____
_____
_____
_____

Who if anyone in my immediate circle can help: _____

_____
_____
_____
_____
_____

Steps I need to take to complete my goal:

_____
_____
_____
_____
_____

How I know that I accomplished my goal:

_____
_____
_____
_____
_____

February

My Goal for this month is:

_____
_____
_____
_____
_____

Who if anyone in my immediate circle can help:

_____
_____
_____
_____
_____

Steps I need to take to complete my goal:

_____
_____
_____
_____
_____

How I know that I accomplished my goal:

_____
_____
_____
_____
_____

March

My Goal for this month is:

_____
_____
_____
_____
_____

Who if anyone in my immediate circle can help:

_____
_____
_____
_____
_____

Steps I need to take to complete my goal:

_____
_____
_____
_____
_____

How I know that I accomplished my goal:

_____
_____
_____
_____
_____

April

My Goal for this month is:

_____
_____
_____
_____
_____

Who if anyone in my immediate circle can help:

_____
_____
_____
_____
_____

Steps I need to take to complete my goal:

_____
_____
_____
_____

How I know that I accomplished my goal:

_____
_____
_____
_____

May

My Goal for this month is:

_____
_____
_____
_____
_____

Who if anyone in my immediate circle can help:

_____
_____
_____
_____
_____

Steps I need to take to complete my goal:

_____
_____
_____
_____
_____

How I know that I accomplished my goal:

_____
_____
_____
_____
_____

June

My Goal for this month is:

_____
_____
_____
_____
_____

Who if anyone in my immediate circle can help:

_____
_____
_____
_____
_____

Steps I need to take to complete my goal:

_____
_____
_____
_____

How I know that I accomplished my goal:

_____
_____
_____
_____

July

My Goal for this month is:

_____
_____
_____
_____
_____

Who if anyone in my immediate circle can help:

_____
_____
_____
_____
_____

Steps I need to take to complete my goal:

_____
_____
_____
_____

How I know that I accomplished my goal:

_____
_____
_____
_____

August

My Goal for this month is:

_____
_____
_____
_____
_____

Who if anyone in my immediate circle can help:

_____
_____
_____
_____
_____

Steps I need to take to complete my goal:

_____
_____
_____
_____
_____

How I know that I accomplished my goal:

_____
_____
_____
_____
_____

September

My Goal for this month is:

_____
_____
_____
_____
_____

Who if anyone in my immediate circle can help:

_____
_____
_____
_____
_____

Steps I need to take to complete my goal:

_____
_____
_____
_____

How I know that I accomplished my goal:

_____
_____
_____
_____

October

My Goal for this month is:

_____
_____
_____
_____
_____

Who if anyone in my immediate circle can help:

_____
_____
_____
_____
_____

Steps I need to take to complete my goal:

_____
_____
_____
_____
_____

How I know that I accomplished my goal:

_____
_____
_____
_____
_____

November

My Goal for this month is:

_____
_____
_____
_____
_____

Who if anyone in my immediate circle can help:

_____
_____
_____
_____
_____

Steps I need to take to complete my goal:

_____
_____
_____
_____

How I know that I accomplished my goal:

_____
_____
_____
_____

December

My Goal for this month is:

_____
_____
_____
_____
_____

Who if anyone in my immediate circle can help:

_____
_____
_____
_____
_____

Steps I need to take to complete my goal:

_____
_____
_____
_____
_____

How I know that I accomplished my goal:

_____
_____
_____
_____
_____

Ok, let me tell you all a little story about me and goal setting. I have never used a list before or wrote my goals out until recently. Yes, you read it write I did not write any of my goals down until about 2015. Before that time, I used to just have it in my mind this is what I am going to do and then I would just get it done. Now as I got older, I started to forget things and little ideas or notions I have so I was forced to utilize pen and paper. I say this to let you all know it is OK to not want or feel like writing things down. As long as you have a strong mind set to continue on towards that path to accomplishing that goal in your mind. If you do not have a strong mindset or you are easily distracted, I suggest you utilize the goal planner I provided or just plain old pen and paper honey.

You see, when I was younger there was not many things to distract me from accomplishing my goals or shall I say I did not let or allow many things to distract me from my goals. I contribute this to age and having less responsibility or things to worry about at that time in my life. To be honest I do not think things started getting in my way of accomplishing goals or needing to write things down until my life got a little more complicated. It was not until I started including relationships, became a single mother, and realizing my parents were getting of age where major health issues came into play. Before then, if I set my mind on something that was my complete focus no matter what I did or no matter what happened. I was hell bent on completing what I started.

Now fast forward to 2018 I have bills, I have a child, I have a career, and I have responsibilities. I need to balance all this with accomplishing my goals and day to day responsibilities. I now have been forced to write things down because it is so easy to forget things or lose focus with trying to make sure the rent and utilities are paid, ensuring your child gets to school on time, making sure she passed all her classes, and all while being in the helping field. It can get exhausting and some days I just lose focus. Gone are the days that I would say to myself I am going to obtain this degree and I am able to just go with the flow. No, I need a plan, I have to have certain things in place for me to obtain this degree like how will I continue to bring in income or who is going to watch my daughter while I am in class? You get my drift. So now I completely understand the reason people write things down because some of us have a lot of things going on in our lives that it becomes so easy for us to lose focus or forget what we are working towards. Writing things down gives us the ability to go back and look at things and remind ourselves of what we are actually working towards and the things we need to get done to accomplish our goals. So, if you are like me and have a busy personal life I urge you to write those ideas down as soon as they come to mind, write your goals out for the month, check them off as you accomplish them, so you can keep track of your progress.

"Every talent you have is not wasted. It is there because of a reason and God will open that door when the right time comes along to use it."

-Shannon L Alder

Timing Is Everything

Timing is everything. We all have heard that phrase more than once in our life. But the saying is so true; sometimes things fall apart, fall through, don't happen, or don't work out how you wanted it to work out simply because it is not your time. We must realize that in life we get the things we prepare ourselves for and sometimes in our mind we are so ready and simply cannot understand why something you want so bad to happen has not occurred. It's simple; the timing is off.

I was facilitating a substance abuse recovery group and one of the participants made a statement that made me look at timing in a whole different light. The participant stated, "We have to learn to submit to our when and our win." Meaning that you will win when it is your time to win and not a moment before that time. And until then you cannot do anything about it but keep pushing and moving forward until you get to where you know you should have been all along.

Today I want you to start looking at your losses in another light. Instead of feeling down or starting the "Oh Why Not Me" party, start saying something like this:

- It wasn't my time to obtain that contract
- He was just not my one, God has something better for me
- Better is coming, it's ok
- It just was not for me

Changing the way you will accept a loss of any kind into a positive light will lessen the chance of you allowing the loss to affect you in a detrimental way. And with anything, practice makes perfect, so you need to begin this as soon as possible. Tomorrow, the first thing you view as a loss, I challenge you to put it in a positive way, such as "Not yet" "It wasn't my time." You can even use the notes and ideas section following this chapter to write it down. Sometimes writing thing down help us get our thoughts and emotions out. Writing it down is much better than suppressing them and never acknowledging your feelings.

Another misconception we tend to use is looking at others. While you are trying to accomplish a goal, or get things started you may feel that you are a failure watching people on Instagram, Facebook, and other social media outlets post all their accomplishment. You may start to think *I'm thirty-five, she's twenty-five and she is making millions;* honey it was her time. Wait on it, your time is coming. Don't get discouraged looking at others glow up. Let it motivate you to create your own glow up. When you're pursuing these social media outlets, you need to be thinking, if she or he can do it so can I! And while you wait on your time always remember delay does not mean denial, your time is coming it just may not be now.

Notes and Ideas

"Gratitude unlocks the fullness of life. It turns what we have into enough, and more. It turns denial into acceptance, chaos to order, confusion to clarity. It can turn a meal into a feast, a house into a home, a stranger into a friend.
-Melody Beattie

<u>Being Grateful</u>

When we go through our tough times in life, it's hard for us to recognize the positives or we even forget the things we have in our life to be grateful for. When we are going through tough times, our first reaction sometimes is to focus on the negative or what happened/what went wrong. But when we force ourselves to look at situations in a positive way or to take a positive out of a stressful situation, we start to internalize and look at the situation in a different way.

I included this exercise for the sole purpose of making you remember good times or positive things in your life. My hopes are when you are down and out, you can look at the list and it put a smile on your face or even shifted your mood. I too, have a list and on mornings I wake up feeling down and just not ready for the world, I get my little list, burn my sage, and smile. You can complete the list prior to a stressful situation or complete the list when you are in the mist of the situation; it's your decision. I have my list ready for my bad days because it is easier for me. Remember, the objective of this exercise is to identify the positives in your life.

Life's Blessings

1. Best Thing that have happened to me:

    _____

2. Most prized possession:

    _____

3. Best things about life:

    _____

4. Favorite Food:

    _____

5. Favorite Drink:

    _____

6. Favorite place to be:

    _____

7. Places I want to go:

    _____

8. Hobbies:

    _____

9. Favorite Sports:

    _____

10. Favorite Television show/movie:

    _____

11. Favorite book/magazine:

    _____

12. Best Physical Feature:

    _____

13. Best Memory:

    _____

14. Past achievement:

    _____

    _____

15. Best Talent:

_____

16. Best Friend/ Family member:

_____

17. Why is it important to focus on the positives?

_____

18. What did you learn about yourself from this activity?

_____

_____

Notes and Ideas

"Writing means sharing. It's part of human condition to want to share-thoughts, ideas, and opinions.

-Paulo Coelho

Emotions and Writing

Sometimes we have feeling, thoughts, emotions, and words that we just cannot say. Whether it's someone we love or even in a career choice. When this happens, sometimes we tend to hold our thoughts to ourselves and at times it causes us stress, anxiety, and worry with thoughts of, "I should have said this" or "I should have told him/her this." This is where writing comes into play; writing will allow you to express yourself without having to re-visit the situation or feeling like or appearing to be holding on to something that everyone else is over.

I personally use this exercise a lot. Believe it or not, I have a hard time expressing myself especially in personal or intimate situations. I can talk all day in my profession but when it comes to expressing my feelings, I always feel as if I left something out. So, I started writing my thoughts when I feel like saying one more thing or if I need closure on a situation or conversation that is now over. Writing my thoughts down provide me with an out let when I cannot tell that person at that particular moment. And sometimes after I write it down, I later express that thought to the person when the opportunity presents itself. I try to make it a habit of not re-visiting situations or conversations that both people consider over for the sake of not drawing the whole ordeal out. For me it works better that way and I'm not suppressing my feelings.

In this next exercise I ask that you keep an emotional journal. You are to track how you feel and your thoughts and emotions for thirty days. After thirty days, I want you to write down how the exercise made you feel. Who knows, after doing this for thirty days, you might want to keep a journal of your day to day activities and feelings. And remember writing is a good coping skill to relieve stress.

Emotion Journal

Day One

Today I feel:

_____

Because:_____

_____

_____

I am excited about:

_____

_____

_____

I am concerned about:

_____

_____

_____

I am hopeful for:

_____

_____

_____

I am thankful for:

_____

_____

_____

I am proud of:

_____

_____

_____

My goal for tomorrow is:

_____

_____

_____

Interesting things about today:

_____

_____

_____

_____

Day Two

Today I feel:

_____

Because:_____

_____

I am excited about:

_____

_____

I am concerned about:

_____

_____

_____

I am hopeful for:

_____

_____

I am thankful for:

_____

_____

I am proud of:

_____

_____

My goal for tomorrow is:

_____

_____

Interesting things about today:

_____

_____

_____

_____

Day Three

Today I feel:

_____

Because:_____

_____

_____

I am excited about:

_____

_____

_____

I am concerned about:

_____

_____

_____

I am hopeful for:

_____

_____

I am thankful for:

_____

_____

_____

I am proud of:

_____

_____

_____

My goal for tomorrow is:

_____

_____

_____

Interesting things about today:

_____

_____

_____

_____

Day Four

Today I feel:

_____

Because:_____

_____

I am excited about:

_____

_____

I am concerned about:

_____

_____

_____

I am hopeful for:

_____

_____

I am thankful for:

_____

_____

I am proud of:

_____

_____

_____

My goal for tomorrow is:

_____

_____

_____

Interesting things about today:

_____

_____

_____

_____

Day Five

Today I feel:

_____

Because:_____

_____

I am excited about:

_____

_____

I am concerned about:

_____

_____

I am hopeful for:

_____

_____

I am thankful for:

_____

_____

I am proud of:

_____

_____

My goal for tomorrow is:

_____

_____

Interesting things about today:

_____

_____

_____

_____

Day Six

Today I feel:

_____

Because:_____
_____

I am excited about:
_____
_____

I am concerned about:
_____
_____
_____

I am hopeful for:
_____
_____

I am thankful for:
_____
_____

I am proud of:
_____
_____
_____

My goal for tomorrow is:
_____
_____

Interesting things about today:
_____
_____
_____
_____

Day Seven

Today I feel:

_____

Because:_____

_____

I am excited about:

_____

_____

I am concerned about:

_____

_____

_____

I am hopeful for:

_____

_____

I am thankful for:

_____

_____

I am proud of:

_____

_____

My goal for tomorrow is:

_____

_____

Interesting things about today:

_____

_____

_____

_____

Day Eight

Today I feel:

_____

Because:_____

_____

_____

I am excited about:

_____

_____

_____

I am concerned about:

_____

_____

_____

I am hopeful for:

_____

_____

I am thankful for:

_____

_____

_____

I am proud of:

_____

_____

_____

My goal for tomorrow is:

_____

_____

_____

Interesting things about today:

_____

_____

_____

_____

Day Nine

Today I feel:

_____

Because:_____

_____

I am excited about:

_____

_____

I am concerned about:

_____

_____

_____

I am hopeful for:

_____

_____

I am thankful for:

_____

_____

I am proud of:

_____

_____

_____

My goal for tomorrow is:

_____

_____

_____

Interesting things about today:

_____

_____

_____

_____

Day Ten

Today I feel:

_____

Because:_____

_____

_____

I am excited about:

_____

_____

_____

I am concerned about:

_____

_____

_____

I am hopeful for:

_____

_____

_____

I am thankful for:

_____

_____

_____

I am proud of:

_____

_____

_____

My goal for tomorrow is:

_____

_____

_____

Interesting things about today:

_____

_____

_____

_____

Day Eleven

Today I feel:

_____

Because:_____

_____

I am excited about:

_____

_____

I am concerned about:

_____

_____

_____

I am hopeful for:

_____

_____

I am thankful for:

_____

_____

I am proud of:

_____

_____

_____

My goal for tomorrow is:

_____

_____

_____

Interesting things about today:

_____

_____

_____

_____

Day Twelve

Today I feel:

_____

Because:_____

_____

I am excited about:

_____

_____

I am concerned about:

_____

_____

_____

I am hopeful for:

_____

_____

I am thankful for:

_____

_____

I am proud of:

_____

_____

_____

My goal for tomorrow is:

_____

_____

Interesting things about today:

_____

_____

_____

_____

Day Thirteen

Today I feel:

_____

Because:_____

_____

I am excited about:

_____

_____

I am concerned about:

_____

_____

_____

I am hopeful for:

_____

_____

I am thankful for:

_____

_____

I am proud of:

_____

_____

_____

My goal for tomorrow is:

_____

_____

_____

Interesting things about today:

_____

_____

_____

_____

Day Fourteen

Today I feel:

_____

Because:_____
_____
_____

I am excited about:
_____
_____
_____

I am concerned about:
_____
_____
_____

I am hopeful for:
_____
_____

I am thankful for:
_____
_____

I am proud of:
_____
_____
_____

My goal for tomorrow is:
_____
_____
_____

Interesting things about today:
_____
_____
_____
_____

Day Fifteen

Today I feel:

_____

Because:_____

_____

I am excited about:

_____

_____

I am concerned about:

_____

_____

_____

I am hopeful for:

_____

_____

I am thankful for:

_____

_____

I am proud of:

_____

_____

_____

My goal for tomorrow is:

_____

_____

Interesting things about today:

_____

_____

_____

_____

Day Sixteen

Today I feel:

_____

Because:_____

_____

I am excited about:

_____

_____

I am concerned about:

_____

_____

_____

I am hopeful for:

_____

_____

I am thankful for:

_____

_____

I am proud of:

_____

_____

_____

My goal for tomorrow is:

_____

_____

_____

Interesting things about today:

_____

_____

_____

_____

Day Seventeen

Today I feel:
_____

Because:_____
_____
_____

I am excited about:
_____
_____

I am concerned about:
_____
_____
_____

I am hopeful for:
_____
_____

I am thankful for:
_____
_____

I am proud of:
_____
_____
_____

My goal for tomorrow is:
_____
_____
_____

Interesting things about today:
_____
_____
_____
_____

Day Eighteen

Today I feel:

_____

Because:_____

_____

I am excited about:

_____

_____

I am concerned about:

_____

_____

I am hopeful for:

_____

_____

I am thankful for:

_____

_____

I am proud of:

_____

_____

My goal for tomorrow is:

_____

_____

Interesting things about today:

_____

_____

_____

_____

Day Nineteen

Today I feel:

_____

Because:_____

_____

I am excited about:

_____

_____

I am concerned about:

_____

_____

_____

I am hopeful for:

_____

_____

I am thankful for:

_____

_____

I am proud of:

_____

_____

My goal for tomorrow is:

_____

_____

Interesting things about today:

_____

_____

_____

_____

Day Twenty

Today I feel:

_____

Because:_____

_____

I am excited about:

_____

_____

I am concerned about:

_____

_____

_____

I am hopeful for:

_____

_____

I am thankful for:

_____

_____

I am proud of:

_____

_____

_____

My goal for tomorrow is:

_____

_____

_____

Interesting things about today:

_____

_____

_____

_____

Day Twenty-One

Today I feel:
_____

Because:_____
_____

I am excited about:
_____
_____

I am concerned about:
_____
_____
_____

I am hopeful for:
_____
_____

I am thankful for:
_____
_____

I am proud of:
_____
_____

My goal for tomorrow is:
_____
_____

Interesting things about today:
_____
_____
_____
_____

Day Twenty-Two

Today I feel:

_____

Because:_____
_____

I am excited about:
_____
_____

I am concerned about:
_____
_____
_____

I am hopeful for:
_____
_____

I am thankful for:
_____
_____

I am proud of:
_____
_____
_____

My goal for tomorrow is:
_____
_____
_____

Interesting things about today:
_____
_____
_____
_____

Day Twenty-Three

Today I feel:

_____

Because:_____

_____

I am excited about:

_____

_____

I am concerned about:

_____

_____

_____

I am hopeful for:

_____

_____

I am thankful for:

_____

_____

I am proud of:

_____

_____

My goal for tomorrow is:

_____

_____

Interesting things about today:

_____

_____

_____

_____

Day Twenty-Four

Today I feel:

_____

Because:_____

_____

I am excited about:

_____

_____

I am concerned about:

_____

_____

_____

I am hopeful for:

_____

_____

I am thankful for:

_____

_____

I am proud of:

_____

_____

_____

My goal for tomorrow is:

_____

_____

_____

Interesting things about today:

_____

_____

_____

_____

Day Twenty-Five

Today I feel:

_____

Because:_____

_____

I am excited about:

_____

_____

I am concerned about:

_____

_____

_____

I am hopeful for:

_____

_____

I am thankful for:

_____

_____

I am proud of:

_____

_____

_____

My goal for tomorrow is:

_____

_____

Interesting things about today:

_____

_____

_____

_____

Day Twenty-Six

Today I feel:

_____

Because:_____

_____

I am excited about:

_____

_____

I am concerned about:

_____

_____

_____

I am hopeful for:

_____

_____

I am thankful for:

_____

_____

I am proud of:

_____

_____

_____

My goal for tomorrow is:

_____

_____

_____

Interesting things about today:

_____

_____

_____

_____

Day Twenty-Seven

Today I feel:

_____

Because:_____

_____

I am excited about:

_____

_____

I am concerned about:

_____

_____

_____

I am hopeful for:

_____

_____

I am thankful for:

_____

_____

I am proud of:

_____

_____

_____

My goal for tomorrow is:

_____

_____

Interesting things about today:

_____

_____

_____

_____

Day Twenty-Eight

Today I feel:
_____

Because:_____
_____

I am excited about:
_____
_____

I am concerned about:
_____
_____

I am hopeful for:
_____
_____

I am thankful for:
_____
_____

I am proud of:
_____
_____

My goal for tomorrow is:
_____
_____

Interesting things about today:
_____
_____
_____
_____

Day Twenty-Nine

Today I feel:

_____

Because:_____

_____

_____

I am excited about:

_____

_____

I am concerned about:

_____

_____

_____

I am hopeful for:

_____

_____

I am thankful for:

_____

_____

I am proud of:

_____

_____

_____

My goal for tomorrow is:

_____

_____

_____

Interesting things about today:

_____

_____

_____

_____

_____

Day Thirty

Today I feel:

_____

Because:_____

_____

I am excited about:

_____

_____

I am concerned about:

_____

_____

_____

I am hopeful for:

_____

_____

I am thankful for:

_____

_____

I am proud of:

_____

_____

_____

My goal for tomorrow is:

_____

_____

_____

Interesting things about today:

_____

_____

_____

_____

_____

Notes and Ideas

"Once you replace negative thoughts with positive ones, you will start having positive results."
-Willie Nelson

Positive Vibes Only

Positive mindset, positive words, positive thoughts, and positive vibes are the main focuses for this time in your life. Remaining positive and always looking for the good in every situation can help you get over the hurdles in life. When things happen, always look to find the positive in the situation rather concentrate on the negative.

One way to start turning all your negative thoughts into positive thoughts is daily affirmation or a daily devotional book. I'm sure many of you may have watched the TV series _Being Mary Jane_. If you recall she has post-it's all over her mirror. Those post-its have daily affirmations or positive words that inspire or encourage her. Those post-it's are something she reads daily when she wakes up to shift her mood. And that's exactly what you will need during a time when you are not feeling your best. I challenge you to put post-its of positive thoughts or words that help you shift your mood. Read them daily before leaving your house to encourage you to remain positive. I have a very bad habit of worrying or over thinking any or everything. Last year some time, I taped an index card on my mirror with the words, "It will be what it's going to be, worry about nothing; pray about everything Philippians 4:6." That's my daily reminder to not worry about things I cannot control because worry causes anxiety and stress, which is not healthy for the mind or body.

I also read a daily devotional every morning before I get out of bed. The first thing I grab is my daily devotional and read the passage for the day. Sometimes I read it twice. If you are having a hard time staying positive, I suggest you get to writing daily affirmations that breathe life into you as well as invest in some good daily devotionals to help you along the way. Below is a list of daily devotionals that I suggest you start with:

- **Where is my Peace by Nako**
- **The Audacity To Be Great by M.D. Hollingshed**
- **Power Thoughts Devotional by Joyce Myers**

Notes and Ideas

"Music is amoral law. It gives soul to the universe, wings to the mind, flight to the imagination, and charm and gaiety to life and everything."
                                        -Plato

Music and Emotions

I know some are reading and saying Music and Emotions???? Well I'm here to tell you yes music can bring different emotions out of you. The tempo in the music can evoke a certain mood or emotions. For instance, if it's a fast tempo it may bring out the happy, excited, or the angry but if it's a slow tempo it may bring out sadness or bring out crying in you. It really depends on the situation and what is going on at the moment. So yes, music can trigger your mood, memory, and your emotions.

For example, when you are getting ready to go out with your friends you are probably not listening to Keyshia Cole's first album; you are probably bumping some Future, Fabolous, or Cardi B. You get my point? So, I say this so you can be mindful of what you are listening to when you are going through different things in life. Going through a break up, don't go turn on no Heather Hedley I'm on an *Emotional Roller Coaster*. All that is going to do is have you sitting up in your room thinking about him like Brandy. Had a bad day at work, don't jam to Kelis *I Hate You So Much Right Now*, you might end up quitting with no source of income. When times are hard, or you are going through something, attempt to listen to music that feeds your soul, and calms your mind. Pick songs that breathe life into you not songs that will keep you in a depressed or angry state.

I want to help you prepare for these times because we all have these times in our life. I have a few songs that I listen to when I need a boost of energy or a change of mood. I have my little playlist ready for when I have rough days. So below I want you to list all the songs that put you in a great mood. Here are some of the songs that I have on my play list, don't judge me because they go from gospel to old rap songs from when I was growing up lol.

- Be Blessed by Yolanda Adams
- The Storm is over now by Kirk Franklin
- I'm Still Standing by Monica
- Fine by Mary J. Blige
- Trials of Love Feat. BK by Prodigy (I really love her part)
- Conceited by Remy Ma
- It's the God in Me by Mary Mary
- Strength of a Woman album by Mary J Blige

That's just a few to give you and idea. You don't have to include gospel, you can just mix all genres. Just make sure the music speaks to your soul and puts you in a great mood.

My Playlist

Notes and Ideas

"Happiness cannot be traveled to, owned, earned, worn or consumed. Happiness is the spiritual experience of living every minute with love grace and gratitude."
-Denis Waitley

Finding Your Happiness

You read right; you cannot buy happiness, you cannot travel to happiness, you cannot borrow happiness, and you damn sure cannot consume happiness. Your happiness can only be found with you and with-in you. A lot of times we mistake happiness based on having certain material things, being with a certain person, having popularity, or living a certain life. But in all actuality, your happiness lies with-in you. I am here to tell you can have all the money in the world, be married to the best man on earth, and have a million followers on all your social media outlets and still be miserable. Material things and tangible items does not equate to a person's happiness, if so do you think we would have celebrities who commit suicide.

You may be reading this asking yourself _well what brings me happiness_? Happiness is different for everyone but what I feel defines a person happiness is when they are totally at peace with themselves. When I say at peace, I mean you are comfortable with your decisions and choices you are making, you are comfortable being by yourself or in a relationship, you're comfortable with not having it all, and you're comfortable with not being on the scene every night and can enjoy your own company at home. For me happiness equates peace, you're mentally healthy, you're spiritually healthy, you're emotionally healthy, and you're physically happy. When you reach that point in your life, you are truly happy. When no one or nothing can steal your joy, you are truly happy. Happiness is the peace that you find with-in yourself. And no one or nothing can tell you how to find that peace or happiness but you. You have to take some time to yourself and really evaluate what makes you happy. And if you feel that you are confused and do not know where to start I provided an exercise below to help you brainstorm ideas on how to make you happy. This exercise is not the end all to be all, but it is the catalyst to start your mind to think about how your happiness looks.

Write a list of things that make you happy:

_____
_____
_____
_____
_____
_____
_____
_____
_____
_____
_____
_____

Write a list of things you do daily:

_____
_____
_____
_____
_____
_____
_____
_____
_____
_____
_____
_____

If you are looking at both list and they are different then you need to compare and comply and form another list below:

_____
_____
_____
_____
_____
_____
_____
_____
_____
_____

Enjoy your journey towards happiness!!!!

"At some point you just have to let go of what you thought should happen and live in what is happening."

-Heather Helper

Live

Throughout everything do not forget to live. I know it's hard to live when you're going through some of the most trying times in your life. But I want you to always remember to learn to enjoy the now. You cannot always think about the past or forever plan for the future that you forget to appreciate your now. Where you are today is what is going to help you exceed in your future. So, enjoy your now so you can appreciate your later. Enjoy every down fall celebrate every little win; even if you celebrate it privately or just doing something small for yourself.

I believe sometimes we get so focused on accomplishing our next goal or recovering from hurt, pain, and discouragement that we do not give ourselves credit where credit is due. Take some time for yourself, take a trip or two, or pat yourself on the back because there is always someone in a worse position than you are in right now. You made it through on your worse days; you put a smile on your face and kept it pushing and for that you deserve to live and enjoy life. And for that you deserve to go out there and enjoy life because your better is coming. So, the next time your friend calls you for dinner or a girls night out, say yes or when that fine specimen asks you out on a date, say yes even if you are not in the mood. Do things that you never thought you would do; accept invitations; do whatever puts a smile on your face because as long as you are smiling you are living.

And if you are having a hard time trying to live you can always revert back to your getting back to me list to help you start living your best life.

Notes and Ideas

Notes and ideas continued

Take Away's

Although I have provided you with various coping strategies throughout this book, I wanted to end it with a few other safe coping skills that are sometimes immediate reactions to different life situations. This list is not inclusive, and I have provided space for you to add extras if needed.

- Inspire yourself- Don't wait for someone to encourage you or put a battery in your back. If you do not have anyone to inspire you to be great, then you be your greatest cheerleader.
- Leave a bad scene or situation- You have the right to remove yourself from any situation or person you do not feel is beneficial to your wellbeing.
- Be persistent- Never give up on yourself, especially when it's beneficial to your well being and will help you be a better you.
- Be Honest- secrets and lying ultimately hurt people. Plus you have to continue a lie to keep up with all the lies you have already told. Do yourself a favor and be honest when you can it help heals wounds.
- Cry- yes cry if you have to let it out, the crying and pain will not last forever. It is best to let it out then to hold it inside. The old saying is true what is done in the dark always come to light.
- Chose self- respect- Above all respect yourself and do whatever will help you wake up and look in the mirror and say I'm great no matter what.
- Take care of your body- exercise and eating healthy goes a long way for your mental health.
- Consider your options- In every situation you have options and choices. Choose what benefits you and help you grow.
- Be conscious of your meaning- be mindful of what you live for; is it your kids? Your family? Your parents? What is your purpose in life?
- Do the best you can with what you have- Make the most out of what you have available or with in your reach.
- Set Boundaries- Do not allow people, things, or situations to take advantage of you or still your joy. Use your power of NO!
- Be compassionate to yourself- do not be hard on yourself. Take care of yourself and listen to your body and inner voice when it says it needs rest
- When your facing a choice always chose the hardest route- the road less traveled is always the road to go.
- _____
- _____
- _____
- _____
- _____

Suicide is real if you feel that you are unable to cope with life or no longer want to live you can always contact the suicide prevention help line to find supports with-in your area 1-800-273-8255.

In closing I hope you enjoyed this book and find it helpful. I began writing this book with every person in mind who goes through tough times and does not see a light at the end of the tunnel, because I was once in your shoes. I once felt that things would not get better and doing some of the things I have put in this book helped me to start walking into the light. Once I started to put energy back into myself and no longer giving or feeding into negativity or focusing on the situation, I began to feel better about myself. My hopes are that when you read this book, it provides you with the outlook you need to start focusing on yourself and making your days brighter. I felt that every exercise in this book provides you with an outlet to help express yourself in a positive way. Plus, these exercises helped me get through some of my toughest days. Please feel free to leave comments or reviews, you can even e-mail me personally and tell me your thoughts at anyeaanderson@gmail.com to provide with your thoughts or ideas.

And finally thank you for purchasing this book and taking your time out your busy day and your busy life for reading this book. I hope this book was helpful to get you out your darkness and helped you move forward towards your Glow Up. Follow me on my business page @andersonconsultingncounsaling or @popntalk on Instagram to stay connected and receive updates on the classes and monthly PopNTalk group sessions.

Work Cited

www.Dannypettry.com

Made in the USA
Columbia, SC
07 February 2023

11283950R00087